D1480801

THE LIBRARY OF FUTURE WEAPONRY™

LAND WARFARE OF THE FUTURE

Roderic D. Schmidt

WILLIAMSBURG REGIONAL LIBRARY
7770 CROAKER RD
WILLIAMSBURG, VA 23188
www.wrl.org

JUL   2007

The Rosen Publishing Group, Inc., New York

For Joe

Published in 2006 by The Rosen Publishing Group, Inc.
29 East 21st Street, New York, NY 10010

Copyright © 2006 by The Rosen Publishing Group, Inc.

First Edition

All rights reserved. No part of this book may be reproduced in any form without permission in writing from the publisher, except by a reviewer.

Library of Congress Cataloging-in-Publication Data

Schmidt, Roderic D.
Land warfare of the future / Roderic D. Schmidt.—1st ed.
       p. cm.—(The library of future weaponry)
Includes bibliographical references and index.
ISBN 1-4042-0524-1 (library binding)
1. Infantry drill and tactics—Juvenile literature. I. Title. II. Series.
UD157.S36 2006
355—dc22

                                                                    2005018101

Manufactured in the United States of America

On the cover: An infantry squad equipped with the Future Force Warrior system engages in simulated urban combat.

CONTENTS

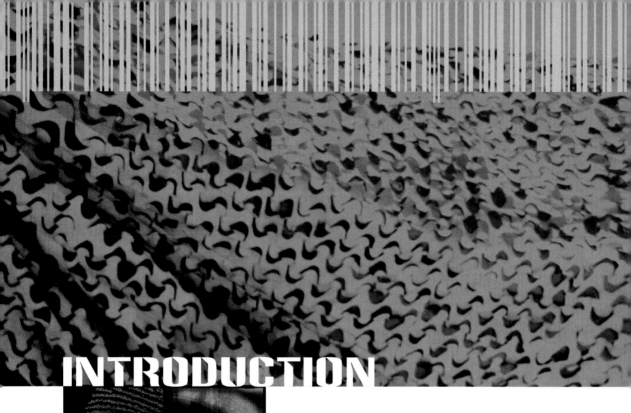

INTRODUCTION

Land warfare has been the most important type of warfare for all of human history. Although nations have learned to wage war in the seas and air, air forces and navies are mainly used to aid ground forces. Most wars are won by taking enemy territory and destroying the enemy's will to fight. Land forces are needed to do both.

Although land forces have always been important, the precise way that they have been used has changed over time. Economic factors influence how large and well-trained an army can be. Technology influences the weapons and tactics an army can use. Politics often determine when and where an army will fight. In the United States, technology and politics have changed a good deal in the past twenty years. The economic strength of the United States and its willingness to spend money on the military has changed to a smaller degree.

The political changes of the past two decades are driving much of the change for the U.S. ground forces. The first big change was the collapse of the Soviet Union in 1991. This removed the enemy that the United States had been preparing to fight since the late 1940s. The United States had placed many heavy, well-armed divisions in Central Europe and elsewhere in case of a Soviet attack. These very deadly but difficult to transport units now had no big enemy to counter.

After the fall of the Soviet Union, the United States reduced the size of its military. Politicians and military leaders felt a large force was no longer needed. As the 1990s progressed, it became clear that a new sort of land force would be needed for the United States to protect itself. New conflicts were likely to use less destructive weapons than the anticipated war with the Soviets. However, wars would also be less predictable and could flare up anywhere. Military units that could be moved quickly became more important than heavy, armored units.

Advances in technology are allowing U.S. military planners to lighten ground forces without sacrificing their effectiveness. The most important advances center around computerized equipment. These new technologies allow units to work closely together and to strike the enemy before the enemy has a chance to strike them. Further into the future, nanotechnology, the science of constructing microscopic robots, is likely to further change land warfare.

The U.S. military is committed to lighter ground forces that use state-of-the-art communications technology to win battles. The army is now in a multistage modernization program. The program is designed to gradually combine the existing heavy forces with the lighter, more experimental forces now coming into service. This will create a highly mobile yet very lethal force that will protect the United States well into the twenty-first century.

NEW IDEAS ABOUT LAND WARFARE

The United States excels in head-on war that involves lots of firepower. Because of this, other nations hesitate to challenge the United States on an open battlefield. Iraq attempted to do so in the 1991 Gulf War and had its military quickly defeated. The Gulf War showed the world exactly how not to fight the U.S. military. Future conflicts are more likely to be smaller-scale wars with the enemy using low-tech weapons. The Battle of Mogadishu in Somalia in 1993 and the current conflict in Afghanistan are two good examples of this sort of engagement.

Many military thinkers are wondering if a military designed for many small conflicts, instead of fewer, larger ones, might work better in the future. The U.S. military has not officially altered its policy yet, but it is under discussion.

U.S. Marines are dropped off by helicopter in an undisclosed location in or near Afghanistan on December 14, 2001. The soldiers were part of Operation Enduring Freedom, the United States' war in Afghanistan following the 9/11 terrorist attacks. In the future, getting soldiers to the battlefield as quickly as possible will be a major goal of the military.

INFORMATION SUPERIORITY

All militaries need accurate information regarding the plans and location of the enemy. The U.S. military is taking the importance of information to another level. The U.S. military wants to have "information superiority" in all conflicts. Information superiority, according to a military publication called *Joint Vision 2010*, is "the capability to collect, process, and disseminate an uninterrupted flow of information while exploiting or denying an adversary's ability to do the same." The U.S. military's plans for the future require consistent information superiority. A great deal of effort and money are being spent to achieve it.

Today, U.S. soldiers have the technology to guide weapons with great precision. In the future, weapons will become even more precise. Information superiority will allow pinpoint strikes that damage only the target and not the homes or businesses of citizens (known as collateral damage).

KNOWING THE BATTLESPACE

The battlespace is where a battle is fought. It includes the land where ground forces clash, the air above, the surrounding sea, and even satellites in space monitoring the entire region. An important goal of the army is to improve what is known as battlespace awareness. An army publication entitled *Transformation Roadmap 2003* defines battlespace awareness as "the ability of joint force commanders and all force elements to understand the environment in which they operate and the adversaries they face." Ideally, this means that both the commanders and soldiers know where everything and everyone that can affect a particular battle is located.

The U.S. military is working to improve battlespace awareness. The lighter units and vehicles of the future will need it in order to be effective. In the past, heavy armor on vehicles was insurance against failure to detect the enemy. If the enemy managed to fire first and hit its target, the vehicle's heavy armor protected it from damage. The lighter forces of the future will not have this insurance. They will need to detect and destroy the enemy before the enemy can bring its weapons into action.

LIGHTENING THE LOAD

The U.S. military is exploring many changes to lighten the weight and increase the speed of units. Some equipment is stationed near potential trouble spots to reduce transport time. For example, the island of Diego Garcia in the Indian Ocean has supplies and weapons that can be moved to the Middle East three weeks quicker than if shipped from the United States. Weight is even saved by simple measures like redesigning ammunition so that it weighs less. It makes little difference with one bullet, but when transporting millions of bullets, it is significant.

Fuel cell technology is being examined as a power source for some military vehicles. This technology could reduce the amount of fuel that needs to be transported to keep military

FINDING A RIDE TO THE BATTLE

There are two ways to transport troops and equipment over long distances to a combat area: by sea and by air. Ship transport is less expensive but has one major disadvantage—it takes a long time. Air transportation is much faster. Because the emphasis in the future will be on speed, all of the military's new vehicles and equipment must be able to fit into C-130, C-17, and C-5 transport planes. If the U.S. military needs to get a unit somewhere quickly, air transport will remain the best way to do it.

The army is beginning to use fuel cell power in some of its vehicles. Fuel cells use hydrogen as an energy source instead of gas or other fuels. In the photograph above, a commander introduces the army's first fuel cell truck. The truck can carry 1,600 pounds (725 kg) and travel at a top speed of 93 miles per hour (150 kilometers per hour).

units running. Fuel cells also give off water as a by-product. This water can be collected and used as drinking water by the unit, reducing the amount of extra water that has to be carried. Small incremental changes such as these all contribute to ground forces that are lighter than ever before.

ROAD MAP FOR THE FUTURE

Former Chief of Staff General Eric Shinseki officially launched the road map for the army of the future in 1999. It envisions multiple forces that will coexist at first and eventually merge into the Future Force sometime around 2032. The Legacy Force consists of the equipment, units, and organization already in

A Stryker Infantry Carrier Vehicle drives off a C-130 transport airplane. The Stryker is one of the vehicles in the army's Interim Force. In the future, all military vehicles will need to be small and light enough to fit inside a C-130. This will allow vehicles to reach the battlefield without having to rely on slower ground or sea transportation.

use by the military. Warfare is too dangerous a business to simply get rid of all the old equipment and ideas and start again. Plus, a threat that requires heavy forces to defeat may reemerge. Because of this, the Legacy Force will be kept around. It will slowly be replaced as new ideas and technologies prove to be reliable.

The Interim Force is a new medium-weight unit. It is transportable by C-130 plane, can operate in any type of combat, and can function in areas with bad roads and rough terrain. The Stryker brigade combat team is the new unit currently making up the Interim Force. The new technologies, organizations, and tactics that the military is developing will be tried and tested by these units.

The knowledge gained from experience with the Interim Force will help determine the shape of the third force, the Future Force. The Future Force will combine the best parts of the Legacy and Interim forces. It will be as lethal and equally protected as the Legacy Force, but it will be quick to deploy, like the Interim Force.

The technologies the Future Force will use are known as the Future Combat Systems (FCS). They are currently in development. The FCS vehicles will be 19-ton (17 metric tons) wheeled vehicles that can be modified for many tasks. The Future Force Warrior is a system of gear, armor, and weapons for infantry. The first of these technologies is expected to begin service by 2010.

INFANTRY

The most basic building block of an army is the infantry. Individual soldiers are the force on the ground that occupies territory and projects a nation's power. Armored vehicles, warships, and warplanes exist to aid the infantry in doing its job. It is rare for military operations not to involve infantry of some sort.

Infantry will continue to play an important role in the twenty-first century, even as future warfare changes. Few forces want to oppose the U.S. military in open warfare. The firepower of the United States is too deadly and effective in open countryside. Future wars are likely to be in cities or very difficult outdoor terrain, where long-range firepower is harder to use. Well-trained and well-equipped infantry is needed to conduct successful operations in such places. The U.S. military is working hard to make sure that the infantry of the army and marines can handle any threat the twenty-first century might reveal.

Right now, the U.S. military is involved in a program to make its infantry much more deadly and tough. The small, personal weapons of the infantry are being upgraded, as well as protective gear and communications equipment. Troops on the ground will be an important part of gaining information superiority. Eventually, it is hoped that everything that each soldier sees will be instantly transmitted across a computer network. This feature will provide commanders with a very current and detailed picture of the battlefield.

LAND WARRIOR

The Land Warrior (LW) system is the first part of the military's program for upgrading the infantry. LW will put together updated weapons, protective equipment and clothing, communications gear, and a personal computer. LW is currently being tested by a limited number of U.S. soldiers. It is scheduled to be regular issue in the army in 2006. The marines and air force are also interested in the program. The goal of Land Warrior is to combine small arms and high-tech equipment to allow U.S. infantry to win on any twenty-first-century battlefield.

M-16A3/M-4

Land Warrior will add electrical components to the M-16A3/M-4 assault rifles. The M-16A3 and M-4 are the assault rifles currently in use by the U.S. military. Both fire 5.56 mm rounds.

A U.S. Army soldier models a proto-type of the new Land Warrior system. The soldier's weapon is a 5.56 mm Colt M-4 assault rifle. Land Warrior will use state-of-the-art tech-nologies to create a soldier who is better protected, better connected to the army's computer network, and more lethal than ever before.

The M-16A3 weighs about seven pounds (three kilograms) and is accurate to a quarter of a mile (400 meters). The M-4 is basically a shortened M-16A3. It weighs a little less but is nearly as accurate as the M-16A3.

Thermal Weapon Sight

A thermal weapon sight (TWS) will allow troops to engage targets in darkness, bad weather, and smoky battlefields. The TWS will also function as a video camera. It will be connected to a tiny eyepiece screen that will enable troops to look and fire around cover while exposing only their hands. A laser

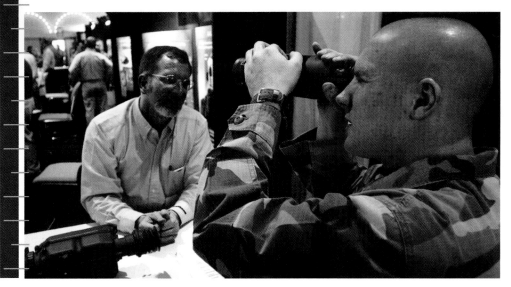

A marine tests a thermal weapon sight (TWS). Sitting across from him is an employee of Raytheon, the sight's manufacturer. The TWS can be mounted on a M-16 or M-4 rifle. It works by detecting the heat given off by a soldier or vehicle. This feature allows it to identify targets at night or in conditions in which it is difficult to see.

rangefinder and digital compass will give troops the precise location and direction of targets.

The thermal weapon sight chosen for Land Warrior is the AN/PAS-13. It has already been used successfully in combat in Iraq.

Computer/Radio Subsystem

The computer/radio subsystem (CRS) will mount to the backpack frame of the LW system. It will include a computer, radio, and a global positioning system (GPS) unit. A handgrip on the soldier's chest will provide control of the CRS and a helmet-mounted display. Soldiers will be able to send digital information over a network to soldiers in their unit as well as up the chain of command. The officer version of the CRS adds a second radio and a flat panel display and keyboard.

Software Subsystem

The software subsystem contains programs to provide the maps, intelligence, and mission data for the CRS. The software can also store video images. It has a power management function to stretch the life of the LW batteries. The software system is designed to be upgradeable so that future improvements can be installed.

Integrated Helmet Assembly Subsystem

Land Warrior's integrated helmet assembly subsystem features a small display screen mounted on the helmet. Soldiers can use it to view the maps, intelligence data, and troop locations stored in the CRS. The images captured with the thermal weapon sight can also be viewed on it. New advanced material will increase protection and comfort while reducing the weight of the subsystem.

Protective Clothing/Individual Equipment Subsystem

The Land Warrior's protective clothing/individual equipment subsystem is built around a new backpack frame design that conforms to the movement of a soldier's body. The frame is also adjustable to minimize fatigue. The LW Interceptor body armor provides greater protection with less weight than current armor. Upgrade plates can be added for use in heavier combat, allowing it to stop small-arms fire from point-blank range. Interceptor armor is already in limited use, but without the other LW subsystems.

FUTURE FORCE WARRIOR

The Future Force Warrior (FFW) is a system of equipment scheduled to appear in 2010. It will use technological advances to make infantry more powerful and also better protected.

XM-8

The XM-8 future combat rifle is designed to replace the M-16A3/M-4. It is the rifle that FFW will likely use. It fires the same 5.56 mm ammunition as the weapons it will replace and is very reliable. It weighs 6.2 pounds (2.8 kg) and is 29.8 inches (76 centimeters) long. It can be quickly and easily customized into four different versions: a general use version, a sharp-shooting version for snipers, an ultracompact shortened version for close-quarters combat, and an automatic rifle variant for more sustained fire.

Many of the devices added on to the M-16A3 and M-4 start out as part of the XM-8. It has a battery-powered sight that includes a red-dot laser for close-range targeting, an infrared laser for aiming in darkness and bad weather, and a laser illuminator for designating targets for laser-guided munitions. These sights do not require the regular readjustments that current sights need. The rifle is designed to allow future improvements so that its service life can be extended.

Soldiers model the Future Force Warrior equipment (right) and the Vision 2020 Future Force Warrior equipment (left). The army hopes to have Future Force Warrior ready for combat in 2010. It will improve upon the weapons, body armor, and communications system being developed for the Land Warrior. The Vision 2020 Future Force Warrior is a project planned for completion in the more distant future. It is in the earliest stages of development.

XM-320

The XM-320 is a grenade launcher that will mount under the barrel of the XM-8. It will fire the 40 mm grenades that are now in use, as well as new 25 mm grenades. The 25 mm grenades have a range of more than half a mile (0.8 km) and variable fuse settings. The variable fuse lets a soldier set the grenade to explode on impact or to burst in the air above a target. The XM-8's laser rangefinder will provide the range to a target, so the fuse can be set to explode exactly where it needs to.

Body Armor

The armor for the FFW will be lighter yet more protective than the Interceptor armor of the LW system. Current body armor can stop a bullet, but the impact will crack ribs and bruise the soldier who has been hit. The hard part of the FFW armor will be 2 to 3 inches (5.1 to 7.6 cm) away from the body. This spacing will reduce the chance of a soldier being injured when struck by a bullet.

Communications System

The communications system of the FFW will allow soldiers to share data with each other and also nearby vehicles and aircraft. This will create a system whereby once one soldier becomes aware of something, it is instantly accessible by everyone on his or her side.

A mannequin models the Future Force Warrior system. Future Force Warrior features a high-tech computer system that is voice-activated. This allows the soldier to keep his hands on his weapon and his eyes on the battlefield at all times.

Computer System

The computer system of the FFW will be voice activated. Data will show up on a clear, eye-level screen attached to the helmet. This heads-up display will let soldiers use their computers without taking their attention away from the battlefield. The computer will also have sensors to monitor a soldier's health. Medics will be able to access this information. The medics can then radio to the injured or sick soldier and give instructions about getting aid.

VISION 2020

The Vision 2020 Future Force Warrior is the most futuristic infantry system being planned. This program is in the idea stage, and it will use some technologies that are only beginning to be developed.

Nanotechnology is the main technology that will make Vision 2020 different than the earlier version of the Future Force Warrior. Nanotechnology involves the construction of materials, devices, and systems that are smaller than 100 nanometers (about one millionth of an inch).

The army hopes to use nanotechnology to create body armor that is soft and flexible but becomes rigid and bulletproof when struck. This armor will also remain effective after multiple hits, unlike current armor that loses protective power after stopping a few bullets. "Nanomuscle fibers" might be embedded in a soldier's uniform to increase strength, speed, and endurance. Nanotechnology may also provide a suit that changes coloration to provide camouflage for a soldier. Medical nanomachines embedded in the soldier's suit to treat wounds by stopping blood loss are planned.

The Vision 2020 Future Force Warrior, as its name suggests, is scheduled to be deployed around 2020. If progress is made with nanotechnology, this will likely happen. Otherwise, the Land Warrior and Future Force Warrior systems will remain in service with upgrades whenever possible.

MILITARY VEHICLES

The armored fighting vehicle (AFV) has been part of the military since the First World War. Armored cars and tanks provide commanders with mobile, protected units with heavy weapons. They are useful for breaking through enemy lines, transporting troops, and many other tasks.

Today, the seventy-ton M1A2 Abrams main battle tank is the backbone of the U.S. Army and Marine armored forces. Its 120 mm gun can be fired on the move and is extremely accurate in all sorts of weather. Its specially designed Chobham armor is nearly invulnerable to all current antitank weapons, and it can reach a speed of 41 miles per hour (66 km/h).

However, the Abrams is also rather noisy and gives off a lot of heat, making it more visible to infrared sensors. It

The M2 Bradley fighting vehicle entered army service in 1981. It is used to carry infantry to the battlefield and to fire at the enemy with its mounted cannon, machine gun, and missile launcher. The army is looking to replace the Bradley with a lighter, faster, and more powerful vehicle that will be part of the Future Combat Systems program.

burns fuel quickly—traveling less than 1 mile per gallon (0.4 kilometer per liter)—and requires large fuel supplies. It is also difficult to transport via airplane.

The U.S. military expects to deal quickly with problems taking place all over the world, and the Abrams is just too big for the job. The military has other, lighter AFVs in its inventory, but these vehicles aren't ideal either. The M2 Bradley fighting vehicle is still fairly heavy at 25 tons (23 metric tons).

The old M113 armored personnel carriers and light armored vehicles are still useful but are beginning to show their age. Most important, none of these light AFVs can provide the power and protection the military requires. A new vehicle, the Stryker, has been designed to fulfill the needs of the twenty-first-century military. It is the first new AFV the military has purchased in a decade.

THE STRYKER

The Stryker vehicles are eight-wheeled armored cars of about 19 tons (17 t). There are two types of Stryker: the Infantry Carrier Vehicle and the Mobile Gun System. The Infantry Carrier Vehicle has eight further subtypes, such as mortar carrier, ambulance, and command vehicle. All the different types share many parts, so supply and repair are made simpler. The Stryker can travel at up to 60 mph (97 km/h), and it is well protected against gun and artillery fire.

The Stryker transports and supports a new type of unit called a Stryker brigade combat team (SBCT). The Stryker is equipped to help the SBCT fight in rugged and urban terrain and in the open.

MARINE VEHICLES

The marines have a new vehicle to replace their aging AAVP7A1 Amtracks. These tracked vehicles are amphibious and can transport up to twenty-one marines from a ship to

The Expeditionary Fighting Vehicle (EFV) will be used to carry marines from a ship to the beach. A test version of the vehicle is seen above at a military range in southern California. With a full load of marines, the EFV can travel up to 28 miles per hour (45 km/h) in the water and 45 miles per hour (72 km/h) on land.

beachhead during combat. The Amtrack can continue to operate on land to support combat operations. However, the AAVP7A1 has been in service for more than thirty years, and its performance and maintenance requirements are no longer satisfactory.

The Expeditionary Fighting Vehicle (EFV) is scheduled to replace the Amtrack around 2010. It will weigh 37 tons (34 t) and transport eighteen marines in much the same way the Amtrack does. However, it is much faster on sea than the Amtrack and has a powerful 30 mm cannon. On the ground, the EFV is as fast as the Abrams. Its speed allows it to keep up with and support troops moving inland after an amphibious landing.

The reconnaissance and surveillance version (RSV) of the Future Combat Systems vehicles will be loaded with electronics equipment designed to locate and track enemy targets. The RSV will be extremely durable and able to operate in any weather condition or time of day. The RSV will also be equipped with at least two unmanned aerial vehicles, which it can use to spy on distant enemy territory.

FUTURE COMBAT SYSTEMS

The next generation of armored fighting vehicles is called the Future Combat Systems (FCS) vehicles. The first FCS vehicles should enter limited service in 2008. They will be fully deployed by 2014. The goal is to create a family of fifteen to twenty FCS vehicles that will be customized for different tasks. This will make production and maintenance easier, just as the shared parts of the different Stryker models do. In many ways, the ideas behind the Stryker and the FCS are essentially the same. The main difference is the newer technology in the FCS and the greater number of versions in the FCS family.

None of the FCS models will weigh more than 19 tons (17 t). Their light weight will allow them to be transported by C-130 aircraft. They will have better fuel efficiency than existing vehicles and will be able to move at 60 miles per hour (97 km/h). Their tires will work even when flat, and adjustable suspensions will improve the ride across difficult terrain.

Some of the varieties of FCS vehicles are infantry carrier, a reconnaissance and surveillance vehicle, an ambulance version, a mortar carrier, a 155 mm artillery carrier, a command version, and a combat version with a 120 mm gun. Supply and maintenance versions are planned, as well as a missile carrier. The missile carrier will likely use the Non-Line-of-Sight (NLOS) system of missiles that is detailed in chapter 5. Basically, anything the military needs to put on a combat vehicle will probably end up on the FCS vehicles.

The designers of the FCS vehicles are well aware of the challenge of making a 19-ton (17 t) AFV that is as tough as the 70-ton (64 t) Abrams tank. To do this, three approaches are being used. Improvements in armor will allow protection with less weight. New defenses will reduce the chance of the vehicle getting hit by the enemy. These measures include reducing the amount of heat the AFV gives off. Less heat means the vehicle will be more difficult to detect and strike with a heat-seeking weapon. The FCS vehicles will also use decoys to fool weapon guidance systems. These decoys are usually flares, which

The MULE is an unmanned ground vehicle currently being developed. MULE stands for Multifunctional Utility/Logistics and Equipment Vehicle. The MULE will assist the infantry with carrying gear, detecting mines, and even attacking the enemy with a mounted gun and anti-tank missiles. In the photo above, a model of the MULE is on display at a military facility in Huntington Beach, California.

create a heat source that is greater than that of the vehicle. Finally, the FCS vehicles will have many built-in sensors and reconnaissance features. These features will allow the FCS vehicles to know where the enemy is at all times.

UNMANNED GROUND VEHICLES

The army is considering many different unmanned ground vehicles (UGVs), which are robotic or remotely controlled vehicles. More than 100 designs are currently being examined. Simple UGVs were used in the Second World War for demolition work. They will play an even larger part on the future battlefield.

Machines will perform dull, dirty, and dangerous tasks with increasing frequency. This will keep more troops out of danger and reduce costs for the military. The jobs the military has for UGVs are already known, although the technology for the UGVs themselves is still not perfected.

There are three types of UGVs planned for use with the FCS. One is the Multifunctional Utility/Logistics and Equipment (MULE) vehicle. It will transport supplies and equipment for infantry in the field.

The armed reconnaissance vehicle (ARV) will have combat and reconnaissance versions. ARVs will be used to gather information and assault enemy units in situations that would be extremely dangerous for troops. Positions that are too well defended for humans to attack or survey will now be attacked or surveyed by robots.

The third UGV will be the soldier unmanned ground vehicle. This 30-pound (13.6 kg) robot will be used to investigate buildings in urban combat, and otherwise check out dangerous things and places. It will be customizable with different sensors and perhaps even weapons.

SUPPORT AIRCRAFT

Aircraft have a great effect on ground combat. They play a role similar to artillery in that they drop heavy firepower on important and tough targets to support ground forces. This type of mission is called close air support (CAS). Many aircraft can carry bombs or missiles to fire at ground targets, but the U.S. military has three craft that are most often used in the CAS role.

The aircraft used for CAS missions are not likely to change for some time. However, the way they communicate with ground forces will change somewhat. Currently, ground forces must send requests for CAS up their chain of command. Then the order will go down the chain of command to the crew of the CAS aircraft, who will carry out the mission. This can take some time, especially if the request is handled by more than one service. An example would be an army tank company requesting CAS from an air force A-10 squadron.

The military is in the process of simplifying communication and command between different units and services. According to the Army's *Joint Vision 2010,* the result will be that "each individual warfighter or crew will be bolstered by enhanced connectivity to comrades, supporting elements, and higher commands." These improvements will reduce the time it takes for CAS to arrive at the battle.

A-10 THUNDERBOLT II

The air force's main CAS aircraft is the A-10 Thunderbolt II. The A-10 was first deployed in 1976. Its service life is expected to end around 2028. Tough design and continual improvements have made the A-10 a valuable tool in the U.S. arsenal.

Because CAS aircraft must operate at low altitudes, they must be able to survive antiaircraft fire from enemy ground units. The A-10 is well armored and has a very strong structure. It has a titanium layer around the cockpit to protect the pilot. The gas tanks are filled with a foam that soaks up the fuel but still lets it flow to the engines, so that very little leaks out if a gas tank is hit. The A-10 also has multiple control systems in case one is destroyed. The engines are located on top of the wings to reduce the chance of damage. High speed is not needed for CAS missions, but planes must be able to dodge antiaircraft fire. The A-10 has larger than usual wings so it can maneuver well.

All these features make the A-10 an effective CAS aircraft, but they also make it somewhat ugly. The A-10, while well liked by pilots, has the affectionate nickname of "Warthog." It may not be the prettiest plane, but it can sustain a massive amount of damage and still fly home.

The A-10 weaponry centers on the GAU-8/A 30 mm Gatling gun, which is located in the nose of the plane. It weighs just over 2 tons (1.8 t), can fire up to 4,200 rounds per minute, and is capable of destroying ground vehicles and tanks. In addition to the GAU-8/A, the A-10 carries 8 tons (7.3 t) worth of other weapons under its wings. These weapons include several sizes of guided and unguided bombs, Mark-77 incendiary bombs, AGM-65 Maverick missiles, and AIM-9 Sidewinder missiles. The AIM-9 is used against aircraft, while the other weapons are used against ground targets.

Flares, electronic countermeasure chaff, and jammer pods are usually carried on the wings of the A-10. These devices are used to fool the guidance systems on surface-to-air missiles.

AH-64D

The army's main CAS aircraft is the AH-64D Apache Longbow helicopter. It is an upgraded version of the AH-64A Apache, which was deployed in 1986. The AH-64D is four times more lethal and more than seven times tougher than the AH-64A. It is expected to remain in service until about 2030. It has a chin-mounted M230 30 mm Gatling gun. Although this weapon is smaller then the A-10's GAU-8/A, it is still deadly.

The AH-64D carries a mixture of weapons depending on the mission. Laser-guided AGM-114 Hellfire missiles are used on armored targets. The Hellfire, once it has located its target, can

An AH-64D Apache Longbow hovers in the air in the above photograph. The AH-64D combines stealth and power to become one of those most feared aircraft in the sky. The helicopter is especially good at hunting down enemy tanks and armored vehicles with its laser-guided Hellfire missiles and 30 mm Gatling gun.

guide itself. This "fire and forget" capability allows the helicopter to move behind cover after firing. The 2.75-inch rockets are used on troops and unarmored targets. It can also carry AGM-122 Sidearm missiles, which follow radar waves to destroy enemy radar systems, and AIM-9 Sidewinders for use on other aircraft.

The device that makes the AH-64D so effective is its Target Acquisition and Designation System (TADS). The AH-64D can peek above a hill and do a quick radar scan with its top-mounted radar dome. TADS will then identify up to 128 targets and tell the pilots which ones are most dangerous. The pilot can then decide which targets to engage.

As a defense, the AH-64D pilot uses the features of the terrain to hide behind. Helicopters flying CAS missions often fly very close to the ground, where radar has difficulty finding them. They can also pop up from behind hills and buildings, attack, and then hide again. This ability makes the AH-64D a feared opponent.

The AH-64D also carries flares and chaff to fool enemy missiles. It has strong armor that can withstand 23 mm anti-aircraft fire.

SUPER COBRA

The U.S. Marines' CAS aircraft is the AH-1W Super Cobra helicopter. It entered service in 1985. It is scheduled to be upgraded to the AH-1Z configuration in 2006. The AH-1Z is likely to remain in service for many years.

The AH-1W carries a 20 mm Gatling gun in a chin mount to attack lightly armored targets. It also carries the AGM-114 Hellfire, AIM-9 Sidewinder, AGM-122 Sidearm, BGM-71 TOW, 127 mm Zuni rocket, and 2.75-inch rockets. The BGM-71 is a guided missile for use on armored targets, like the Hellfire. The BGM-71 is unlike the Hellfire in that the helicopter must remain exposed while guiding it to the target. The 127 mm Zuni rockets are used against troops and unarmored targets. The AGM-114, AIM-9, and AGM-122 are used in the same ways that the AH-64D uses them.

To protect itself, the AH-1W hides behind terrain features. It also has flares and chaff to fool enemy infrared- and radar-guided

A test version of the AH-1Z Super Cobra attack helicopter lifts off from a military base in Maryland. The AH-1Z will be able to carry twice as much weaponry and gear as the AH-1W version of the Super Cobra can. However, the AH-1Z will share many of the features of the existing Super Cobra in order to save money.

missiles. The AH-1Z will get a Cobra Radar System, which is a version of the radar system used in the army's AH-64D.

UNMANNED COMBAT AERIAL VEHICLES

In coming decades, manned CAS aircraft will likely be joined by unmanned combat aerial vehicles (UCAVs). These remotely controlled aircraft are less expensive to construct than manned aircraft. They can also be used to avoid risking the lives of pilots in extremely dangerous missions.

Antiaircraft missiles are a great danger to CAS aircraft. Even with the many protective measures taken, CAS missions may

The X-50 unmanned combat aerial vehicle is also known as the Dragonfly. It is 17.7 feet (5.4 m) long and 6.5 feet (2.0 m) wide, with a rotating blade measuring 12 feet (3.7 m) across. At least two X-50s have already been built and are being tested for performance and reliability.

become impractical if antiaircraft weapons continue to become more effective. Because they are relatively cheap and replaceable, UCAVs are probably going to take over more of this sort of mission in the future.

The RQ-1 Predator is a UCAV that has already been used for combat missions. In November 2002, a remotely controlled Predator used a Hellfire missile to destroy a car containing six suspected terrorists in Yemen. The army is working on the X-45 UCAV, and the navy has its version, the X-47. These

UCAVs look like little planes. The Boeing A-160 Hummingbird uses rotor propulsion, like a helicopter, and will be able to carry 300 pounds (136 kg) of sensors or other equipment.

Other UCAVs use new technology. The Boeing X-50 combines the features of a plane and a helicopter. First, it uses a rotating blade called a rotor to take off like a helicopter. Then, the rotor locks in place like a wing so it can travel faster than a typical helicopter. Both manned and unmanned versions of the X-50 are being considered.

The UCAVs will be used for reconnaissance and surveillance, and to attack ground forces, especially enemy antiaircraft artillery units. Operators will control these UCAVs remotely and make decisions on how much force to use.

In many ways, UCAVs will function as a sort of superintelligent missile. They will be able to fly about, gathering information. If the time comes to attack, they can do so without regard to survival. Recovering the UCAV is certainly desirable, but since no pilot is at risk, it is much less important.

STAND-OFF WEAPONS

The infantry, with support from armored fighting vehicles and aircraft, take and hold enemy territory. However, for much of the twentieth century it was the artillery arm that inflicted the most casualties on the enemy. Although the firepower of the infantry squad will increase in the future, the artillery will remain a major weapon on the battlefield.

PROVIDING INDIRECT FIRE

Artillery, also known as stand-off weaponry, helps other ground forces fight through indirect fire. Indirect fire is when a weapon shoots at a target that is not visible. Indirect fire became possible around the turn of the nineteenth century, when guns were invented that could fire shell after shell the same height and distance.

A soldier known as a forward observer identifies a target during an exercise in Iraq in March 2004. During combat, it is the forward observer's responsibility to pass on the location of a target to the artillery unit. The forward observer must be extremely precise with the target coordinates, because any error can lead to accidental civilian death or destruction of civilian property.

Once the military was able to predict where shells would land, artillery could engage targets that were not visible. The system was not perfect; a soldier trained to work with artillery, called a forward observer, would act as the artillery's eyes. Often the first shells would not be right on target, so the forward observer would correct the aim of the artillery unit to get the shells on target. Sometimes artillery would fire without a forward observer at areas thought to conceal enemy troops. Without a forward observer, artillery would generally try to cover a larger area with as much firepower as possible, a type of attack called a barrage.

Indirect fire allows ground units to put heavy firepower on targets that they might not be able to attack otherwise. It also allows artillery to be located safely away from the battlefield. Frontline troops get the power of the artillery without having to carry it themselves.

ADVANCES IN ARTILLERY

The biggest change in the relationship between frontline forces and artillery is the speed with which requests for artillery fire will be carried out. In the past, requests would move up the chain of command by telephone or radio to special units. These special units would plan which artillery units would fire and at what target. They would also make aiming calculations. This could take a while, leaving the frontline units without support fire.

Communications advances and streamlined chains of command will decrease the time for requests to be filled in the future. Computers have already greatly reduced the time needed to make aiming calculations.

Identical shell arcs, maps, and mathematics allow artillery to use indirect fire. The same things allow forces to work backward and figure out where enemy artillery is located. Radar specially designed to plot the arc of artillery shells makes this process very rapid. Once the enemy artillery has been located, it can be fired upon. The result is two sets of artillery firing at each other.

Being able to move and fire from different locations is the best defense against these artillery fights. Because of this, the United States will continue to put many of its artillery pieces on vehicles. This type of artillery is known as self-propelled artillery.

SELF-PROPELLED ARTILLERY

Self-propelled artillery first appeared during the Second World War. The current self-propelled artillery piece for the U.S. Army is the M-109A6 Paladin. It entered service in 1994 and is an upgraded version of a design that dates back to the 1960s. It will likely continue in service until replaced by the artillery variant of the FCS vehicle around 2010.

The Paladin carries a 155 mm gun that can hit targets up to 20 miles (32 km) away. It takes sixty seconds to prepare for firing after coming to a stop. The crew does not need to leave the vehicle to get set up, a requirement of many older self-propelled artillery pieces. The Paladin can move at 40 miles per hour (64 km/h). Its speed, combined with its rapid setup, gives it the "shoot and scoot" capability artillery needs to survive.

The other self-propelled component of U.S. artillery forces is the M270A1 Multiple Launch Rocket System (MLRS). The MLRS is a M2 Bradley fighting vehicle that has been altered to carry twelve M26 rockets. These rockets can carry a cluster of tiny bombs called bomblets. When dropped, the bomblet can cover an area 220 yards (200 m) across. Troops in Iraq nicknamed this shower of bomblets "steel rain."

A test version of the non-line-of-sight cannon (NLOS-C) fires a 155 mm shell in this photograph taken in July 2005. The NLOS-C is the artillery variant of the Future Combat Systems vehicles. It is designed to be able to move fast and fire quickly. The NLOS-C will also be light enough to be carried to distant battlefields inside a C-130 aircraft.

The MLRS can also fire AT2 rockets that scatter antitank mines, as well as the larger, guided Army Tactical Missile System (ATACMS). The ATACMS are larger and can fly farther than the M26. Some versions carry a single explosive charge, while others carry bomblets.

The MLRS is used to put a large amount of firepower on a target very quickly. The MLRS can fire and move rapidly, like the Paladin, to avoid enemy artillery fire. It takes about three minutes to reload the M26 rockets, after which another devastating attack may be launched. The M270 entered service in 1983, and the upgraded M270A1 was issued to troops in 2002. It is likely to remain in use for many years.

NON-LINE-OF-SIGHT LAUNCH SYSTEM

The Non-Line-of-Sight Launch System (NLOS-LS) is a missile system designed as part of the Future Combat Systems. No deployment date is set for the NLOS-LS, although it seems likely to appear with the Future Force Warrior in 2010. The NLOS-LS is designed to work very closely with other units on the battlefield.

In this illustration, two soldiers operate the Non-Line-of-Sight Launch System (NLOS-LS). The box to the right is known as the container launch unit. It can hold up to fifteen missiles. The NLOS-LS is lightweight and easy to transport. It has a sophisticated computer system that allows it to be operated remotely.

The NLOS-LS is a system of two missiles. The loitering attack missile (LAM) will fly over the battlefield, transmitting the locations of targets to a command center. The precision attack missile (PAM) is a guided missile that will attack targets found by the LAMs. The LAM can also be used to attack a target if necessary. LAMs and PAMs share many components to reduce production and maintenance costs.

Both missiles can be launched from either a helicopter or a ground vehicle. The Humvee is being examined as one option. A version of the FCS vehicle that can mount the NLOS-LS is planned as well.

TOWED ARTILLERY

Towed artillery is artillery that is mounted on wheels and requires a vehicle to tow it or troops to carry it. Although the technology is somewhat outdated, it still has a place on the modern and future battlefield.

The M119A1 105 mm howitzer entered service in 1989 and is a light and lethal piece of artillery. It is easily air transportable, weighing a little more than 2 tons (1.8 t). It can hit targets 12 miles (19 km) away.

The M198 155 mm howitzer weighs a little less than 8 tons (7 t), so it can be transported by aircraft. It can hit targets nearly 20 miles (32 km) away with rocket-assisted rounds. The M198, as large as it is, still only takes six minutes to get ready to fire.

U.S. soldiers get ready to fire an M777 howitzer at a test range in the southern California desert. The high-powered but lightweight M777 is the latest addition to the army's imposing collection of towed artillery.

The army and marines have recently added the M777 155 mm howitzer. It weighs less than 5 tons (4.5 t), which fits into the military's plan for easily transportable forces in the future. It can also be ready to fire in only two or three minutes. The M777 can fire five rounds per minute for a short while, or two rounds per minute for extended periods.

UNIT ORGANIZATION AND TACTICS

The military force that the United States created during the decades after World War II is known as the Legacy Force. It was designed for a war with the Soviet Union. The Legacy Force was made up of divisions equipped with the latest tanks and other heavy weaponry. These divisions could generate massive firepower, but they were difficult to move because of all their heavy equipment. However, because the Legacy Force was stationed in Central Europe close to the Soviet Union, the difficulty in transporting these military units was not a problem.

When the Soviet Union collapsed, the United States no longer had to worry as much about fighting a war with the Soviets. Some of the large military forces that had been built up were disbanded because they were no longer needed. The United States also saved money by shrinking

The M1 Abrams tanks have been active in the war in Iraq, also known as Operation Iraqi Freedom. Above, an Abrams returns to its base after a battle in July 2004 in which fifteen Iraqi police officers, two U.S. soldiers, and more than thirty rebels were killed. The Abrams is a deadly but very heavy tank. Since it is difficult to transport, the U.S. Army plans to use lighter armored vehicles in the future.

the military. The types of units in the army did not change much, though. There were just fewer of the high-firepower, difficult to move units.

THE CHANGING FACE OF WAR

As the 1990s progressed, it became clear to U.S. military planners that even though the Soviet Union was no longer a rival, there would still be plenty of small wars that the United States would need to fight. In many of these wars, the combat would be against opponents with weaponry and tactics different from those of enemies of the past. The need to get to the area quickly to influence events would be great. The Balkan War and the intervention in Somalia are two examples of this sort of war. Mobility has increased in importance, while raw firepower has decreased.

Technological advances are allowing the U.S. military to change without sacrificing the strength of its troops. The most important advances are improved communications systems and sensors. These technologies allow rapid, precision strikes against the enemy. They also help U.S. forces work together in close cooperation. New vehicles and equipment are lighter but as effective as the older, heavier items they replace. Right now, the U.S. military is in the process of shifting from one type of force to another. The Legacy Force exists in reduced numbers, and the Interim Force is growing in size and importance. The Future Force is on the not-too-distant horizon.

STRYKER BRIGADE COMBAT TEAMS

To fulfill these plans, in 1999 the U.S. military began developing a new type of unit. These units are organized so that they can be deployed anywhere in the world in ninety-six hours. They make up the Interim Force that the military is using to test new ideas about equipment and tactics. They use the Stryker vehicle, and are called Stryker brigade combat teams (SBCTs).

The SBCTs will provide valuable experience for the Future Force that is being planned. The SBCTs are designed as follow-up forces to be used once the first-in forces (generally marines)

Army soldiers from the 25th Infantry Division Stryker brigade combat team patrol the streets of Mosul, Iraq, on February 14, 2005. The metal tubing that surrounds the Stryker vehicle is armor to protect it from rocket-propelled grenades, which are a popular weapon among the rebel forces in Iraq.

establish a base of operations. Infantry supplies most of the units' firepower, with support provided by the Stryker. The Land Warrior and Future Force Warrior programs will make the SBCTs' infantry very dangerous and tough. Some of the SBCTs were deployed to Iraq in 2004 to gain combat testing and experience.

The SBCT has about 3,600 troops in it. The SBCT has support and field artillery battalions, and intelligence, engineer, and antitank companies as part of its organization. The SBCT has a special unit that helps it stay aware of all enemy activity. This unit is called the reconnaissance, surveillance, and target acquisition battalion.

FUTURE FORCE

The Future Force is the eventual goal of the U.S. military. It will be a light and lethal force that has all the combat ability of the Legacy Force, but it will be easier to transport. The Future Combat Systems (FCS) will be the backbone of this new force. Some of the FCS vehicles were described in chapter 3.

There is also a system of sensors and communications being designed for the FCS that will network the soldiers of the army, navy, marines, and air force. This network, known as the Warfighter Information Network-Tactical (WIN-T) marines, will provide accurate information and battlespace awareness for all soldiers in the armed forces.

In July 2004, the army announced that it is speeding up delivery of some of the FCS vehicles. The plan is to equip the first FCS unit in 2008, with thirty-two brigades equipped by 2014. The following systems have been given priority for the future:

- FCS vehicles equipped with gun and missile artillery

- Ground sensors

- Unmanned aerial vehicles

- Armed robotic ground vehicles

These technologies are important in making the Future Force possible. The FCS artillery vehicles will provide the heavy, long-range firepower needed to engage and destroy opponents

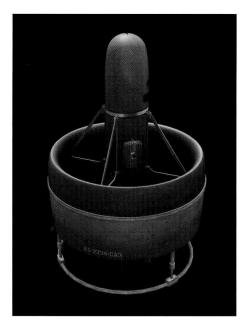

The Future Combat Systems will include a number of unmanned aerial vehicles (UAVs). The illustration at left is a future UAV that will be used by infantry to spy on enemy territory and troops. The UAV will weigh 60 pounds (27 kg) and fit inside a backpack. It will be able to remain in flight for up to sixty minutes.

before they can strike. Sensors and unmanned aerial vehicles are important for locating targets and enemy activity. Armed robots can find targets, attack the enemy, and be used for other dangerous missions without risking the lives of soldiers.

THE GOAL OF THE FUTURE ARMY

The U.S. Army's Web site states that the goal of the future army is to "see first, understand first, act first and finish decisively." The organization of the Future Force will likely be something like the SBCT. It will have many different types of troops as a regular part of its organization. The Future Force will use more robotic and unmanned reconnaissance and surveillance vehicles. More of the offensive firepower will probably be mounted on remotely or robotically controlled vehicles.

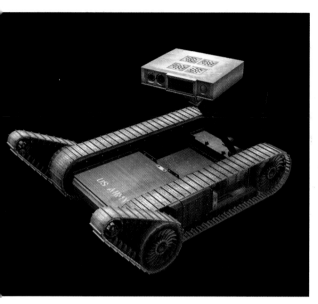

This is an illustration of the Small Unmanned Ground Vehicle (SUGV), which will be part of the Future Combat Systems. The SUGV is designed to work in tight spaces such as caves, tunnels, and sewers. Its job will be to locate enemy forces and to detect dangerous chemicals and explosives.

These unmanned vehicles, in addition to providing information about the enemy and the ability to attack, have another benefit. Such unmanned systems required fewer people to operate and fewer supplies to maintain than similar manned systems. That means less people to train and pay, thus saving money for the United States. It also means that less food, water, fuel, and other supplies need to be shipped to deployed troops. This reduced need for supplies makes it easier to keep units in the field. It also frees up ships and planes from supply missions so they can be used for other tasks.

WHAT DOES THE FUTURE HOLD?

The U.S. military is being very cautious in its transformation. The military is careful not to suddenly get rid of all its old equipment and ideas. If the new equipment and ideas do not work out as planned, the tried and true force is still there to use. Transforming the military must be done in a cautious fashion because a mistake could leave the nation with big defense problems.

It is also important to understand that the performance of the Interim Force (the Stryker brigade combat teams) will greatly influence what happens with the Future Force. If the SBCTs suddenly begin having trouble, the Future Force will likely be changed to fix those problems.

The U.S. military is being very careful in planning for the future. The best technologies, ideas, and people are being employed in the transformation. Great effort is being put forth to make sure that U.S. citizens are protected by the most powerful military in the world.

GLOSSARY

amphibious Capable of operating on land and in water.

battalion Military unit consisting of 500 to 1,200 soldiers.

beachhead Part of a shore held by invading troops, usually as a place from which to begin a larger invasion.

brigade Military unit consisting of 2,000 to 5,000 soldiers.

chaff Strips of foil or lengths of wire ejected into the air to jam enemy radar.

Chobham armor The special armor used on the Abrams tank. It was developed in Chobham, England, and its exact makeup is still a secret.

company Military unit consisting of about 120 soldiers.

deploy To make ready for use.

division Military unit consisting of about 15,000 soldiers.

Gatling gun A machine gun with multiple rotating barrels that allow it to fire at a very fast rate.

incendiary bomb An explosive device designed to start a fire.

jammer pods Devices designed to disrupt enemy radar.

mortar A short-barreled cannon used to send explosives high into the air.

nanometer One billionth of a meter.

reconnaissance The act of checking out an area in person or with sensors to gather information about terrain, layout, and enemy activity.

self-propelled artillery Artillery pieces (cannon or rocket) that are mounted on vehicles.

squad The smallest military unit, consisting of eight to fourteen soldiers.

surveillance The act of secretly watching over known enemy units or territory.

tactics The movement of soldiers and weaponry into the best positions before and during a battle.

towed artillery Artillery (almost always cannon) mounted on wheels that requires a vehicle to tow or carry it if it is to be moved long distances.

tracked vehicle A type of vehicle that uses tracks instead of wheels to move. Examples of tracked vehicles are tanks, bulldozers, and snowmobiles.

FOR MORE INFORMATION

Federation of American Scientists
1717 K Street NW
Suite 209
Washington, DC 20036
(202) 546-3300
Web site: http://www.fas.org

Jane's Information Group
110 North Royal Street
Suite 200
Alexandria, VA 22314
(800) 824 0768
Web site: http://www.janes.com

Web Sites

Due to the changing nature of Internet links, the Rosen Publishing Group, Inc., has developed an online list of Web sites related to the subject of this book. This site is updated regularly. Please use this link to access the list:

http://www.rosenlinks.com/lfw/lawf

FOR FURTHER READING

Evans, Nicholas D. *Military Gadgets: How Advanced Technology Is Transforming Today's Battlefield—and Tomorrow's.* Upper Saddle River, NJ: Financial Times Prentice Hall, 2004.

Foss, Christopher F., ed. *The Encyclopedia of Tanks and Armored Fighting Vehicles.* San Diego, CA: Thunder Bay Press, 2002.

Murray, Stuart. *The Encyclopedia of War and Weaponry.* New York, NY: Franklin Watts, 2002.

Poolos, J. *Army Rangers: Surveillance and Reconnaissance for the U.S. Army.* New York, NY: Rosen Publishing Group, 2003.

Richie, Jason. *Weapons: Designing the Tools of War.* Minneapolis, MN: Oliver Press, 2000.

Sun Tzu. *The Art of War.* New York, NY: Fine Communications, 2004.

Vizard, Frank, and Phil Scott. *21st Century Soldier: The Weaponry, Gear, and Technology in the New Century.* New York, NY: Time, 2002.

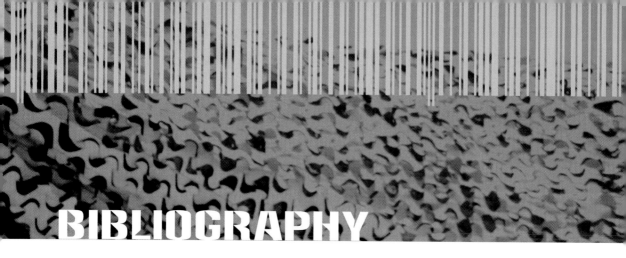

BIBLIOGRAPHY

Bartelt, Eric. "Land Warrior." July 19, 2002. Retrieved March 11, 2005 (http://www.usma.edu/publicaffairs/PV/020719/Warrior.htm).

Berkowitz, Bruce. *The New Face of War: How War Will Be Fought in the 21st Century.* New York, NY: Free Press, 2003.

Binnendijk, Hans, ed. *Transforming America's Military.* Honolulu, HI: University Press of the Pacific, 2002.

Carter, Ashton B., and John P. White, eds. *Keeping the Edge: Managing Defense for the Future.* Cambridge, MA: MIT Press, 2001.

Chairman of the Joint Chiefs of Staff. *Joint Vision 2010: America's Military: Preparing for Tomorrow.* Washington, DC: U.S. Government Printing Office, 2000.

Defense Update. "Future Combat Systems." 2004. Retrieved February 3, 2005 (http://www.defense-update.com/topics/topics-fcs.htm).

Director for Strategic Plans and Policy, J5: Strategy Division. *Joint Vision 2020.* Washington, DC: U.S. Government Printing Office, 2000.

Dunnigan, James F. *Digital Soldiers: The Evolution of High-Tech Weaponry and Tomorrow's Brave New Battlefield.* New York, NY: St. Martins' Press, 1996.

Federation of American Scientists. "United States Weapon Systems." Retrieved April 15, 2005 (http://www.fas.org).

GlobalSecurity.org. "US Weapon Systems." Retrieved April 14, 2005 (http://www.globalsecurity.org/military/systems/index.html).

Miller, David, ed. *The Illustrated Directory of Modern American Weapons.* St. Paul, MN: MBI Publishing, 2002.

O'Hanlon, Michael. *Technological Change and the Future of Warfare.* Washington, DC: Brookings Institution Press, 2000.

Shukman, David. *Tomorrow's War: The Threat of High-Technology Weapons.* New York, NY: Harcourt Brace, 1996.

Space Daily. "A160 Hummingbird Resumes Flight Testing as Boeing UAV." Retrieved June 4, 2005 (http://www.spacedaily.com/news/uav-04zzt.html).

Steed, Brian. *Armed Conflict: The Lessons of Modern Warfare.* New York, NY: Ballantine Books, 2002.

United States Army. "About SBCT." November 7, 2003. Retrieved March 1, 2005 (http://www.lewis.army.mil/transformation/index.asp).

United States Army. *Transformation Roadmap 2003.* Retrieved August 22, 2005 (http://www.army.mil/2003Transformation Roadmap3002).

U.S. Army Natick Soldier Center. "Future Force Warrior." May 19, 2004. Retrieved February 2, 2005 (http://www.natick.army.mil/soldier/WSIT).

Williams, Cindy, ed. *Holding the Line: U.S. Defense Alternatives for the Early 21st Century.* Cambridge, MA: MIT Press, 2001.

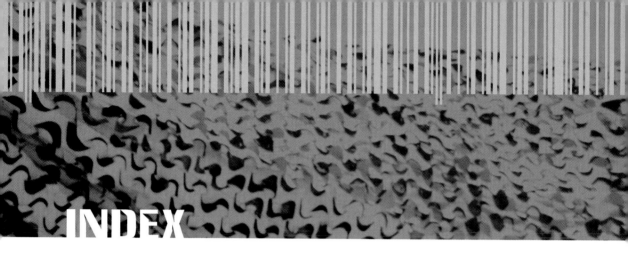

INDEX

About the Author

Roderic D. Schmidt has been fascinated by military matters since seeing a tabletop wargame as an impressionable ten-year-old. Over the years, his interest in the military became a more general interest in history, motivating him to get a BA in history at Trenton State College. He lives in New York City with his wife, Magdalena. He recommends the old *Squad Leader* wargame for those interested in infantry tactics and combat simulation.

Photo Credits

Cover US Army Natick Soldier Center; cover (left corner) © Digital Vision/Getty Images; cover (top middle) © Photodisc Red/Getty Images; pp. 7 and throughout, 8 Chief Photographer's Mate Johnny Bivera/U.S. Marines; p. 11 by courtesy of General Motors/Max Schulte/Photo Courtesy of U.S. Army; pp. 12, 28, 47, 53, 54 Photo Courtesy of U.S. Army; p. 16 © Justin Sullivan/Getty Images; p. 17 © David McNew/Getty Images; pp. 20, 22 Photo by Phil Copeland/U.S. Department of Defense; p. 25 by Department of Defense/ Photo Courtesy of U.S. Army; p. 27 Courtesy of Shawn Haag, General Dynamics/U.S. Marines; p. 30 © Matt Sayles/AP/Wide World Photos; pp. 35, 45 Courtesy of Lockheed Martin; p. 37 Troy Lancaster/Naval Air Systems Command; p. 38 © The Boeing Company; p. 41 U.S. Army photo by Staff Sgt. Joseph Roberts; p. 44 © Getty Images; p. 49 by Staff Sgt. Klaus Baesu/Photo Courtesy of U.S. Army; p. 51 by Sgt. Jeremiah Johnson/Photo Courtesy of U.S. Army.

Designer: Evelyn Horovicz; Editor: Brian Belval

WITHDRAWN

BY
WILLIAMSBURG REGIONAL LIBRARY